EVOLUTION
Who and What Is Man?

Theosophical Manual No. VI

Evolution

Who and What Is Man?

By
HENRY TRAVERS EDGE

POINT LOMA PUBLICATIONS, INC.
P. O. Box 9966
SAN DIEGO, CALIFORNIA, U.S.A. 92109

ISBN: 0-913004-22

Printed in the United States of America by
Stockton Trade Press, Inc.
Santa Fe Springs, California

CONTENTS

EDITORS' PREFACE

Nature exists and Man exists, and somewhere, unobscured by man's own sophistries there must be available the wisdom and learning which tells us *why* and *how*. As we ponder the question it seems an inevitable conclusion that somewhere there must be preserved a recording, a gathering of facts or 'laws', a formulation in human language of the truth concerning Man and Nature. There must be a basic source from which sciences, philosophies and great religions have sprung.

H. P. Blavatsky, in her writings of immense intellectual and spiritual power — still not fully appreciated — points to that living Source, declaring it exists. She called it the Ancient Wisdom, the Sacred Science, the *Gupta-Vidyâ,* and gave to it the Greek name of *Theosophia,* Theosophy, knowledge and wisdom such as the gods or divinities live by. This Ancient Wisdom, she affirmed, has always been in existence, though not always publicly known, having come down the ages tested and checked by generations of Great Seers. It may be called the Facts of Being, the 'laws' or workings of Nature.

In this series of twelve Theosophical Manuals this Ancient Wisdom in its fundamentals is explained with clarity of presentation and logical appeal by students and scholars who have devoted a lifetime to theosophic study. Above all they have been governed by strict honesty and adherence to the teachings as originally reported and recorded.

The first booklet, *Theosophy: A General View of Occult Doctrine,* outlines the over-all teachings, presenting a general picture. Succeeding booklets cover in greater detail the subjects of Reincarnation, Karma, The Seven Principles of Man, Death and the After-Death States of Consciousness, Evolution, Man's Divine Parentage: the Origin of Man and of the Earth, the Doctrine of Cycles, The Ladder of Life: Hierarchies, The Astral Light, Psychic Powers, and Theosophy and Christianity.

It is hoped that these Studies will be received with an open mind, for in them the earnest searcher will find keys that are indispensable to an understanding of the Universe and of Man.

Helen Todd
W. Emmett Small

INTRODUCTORY

THE word evolution is used in Theosophy to denote the universal process by which everything is brought into being; and consequently the subject, if treated in full, would be much too large for a single manual; besides which, the student would be overwhelmed with the vastness of the subject and confused with a mass of details. What we must do therefore is to present a broad outline of the subject as a whole, and to confine our more detailed treatment to special branches of it, such as the evolution of man and the animals, the Darwinian theory, and similar matters of general interest. And this plan will of course involve the making of approximate statements, true as far as they go, yet not the whole truth. In short, we pursue the usual method adopted by students of any science, and that is to begin with an elementary course and leave the higher course to a later time. And, since evolution covers so large a scope, and Theosophy is one whole, frequent references will have to be made to other manuals of this series, which deal specially with other branches of the subject.

Evolution is the universal process by which things change and grow and develop. Its nature can be understood by a few familiar illustrations. A seed is planted, a minute particle, hardly distinguishable from other kinds of seed; but it goes through various stages of development until it has become a fully grown tree with flowers and fruit. This is evolution; the tree has evolved from the seed. A fertilized ovum in the womb passes through many stages until a fully formed human infant is produced, and this again develops until a fully grown human being appears. This again is evolution and the man has evolved from the germ. An architect conceives in his mind an idea; this idea takes form on paper, and plans are drawn; ultimately the plans are executed in marble and granite, until through many stages and by the work of many hands there has arisen a superb and mighty cathedral. This again is evolution and the edifice has evolved from the idea. Human affairs illustrate the same law of evolution; for here we find institutions, social orders, customs, growing up through stages as manifestations of some idea or plan in which they originated. In a word, evolution is the realization of ideals.

There are other ways of defining the meaning. We can say that it means the bringing into visibility of that which was invisible; the bringing into activity of that which was latent; the coming into manifestation of what was unmanifest. But it does *not* mean the creation of anything that did not exist before. The cathedral existed before; not as a stone edifice, but as an idea in the mind of the architect. The tree existed before its physical manifestation; it existed in latency, in potentiality, within the seed. The entire future man was concealed somewhere in or about the germ. Were this not so, there would be nothing to determine why one seed should produce one kind of tree, and another another.

We know that the growing seed gathers to itself elements from earth, air, water, and light; and of these builds its physical structure. The biologist with his microscope can study the evolution of a cell, and give a most elaborate and detailed description of what happens; but he cannot see the agencies at work, and may define them as inherent properties of matter or of some life-principle.

No sense can be made out of the matter until we recognize all these activities as guided by intelligence. Mind, purpose, intelligence, instinct, desire, guide all the processes in nature; and if we do not admit this, we shall be obliged to invent something else which in some mysterious way performs all the results of intelligence. Moreover, the mind, purpose, etc., are the attributes of living beings, and cannot be thought of apart from the living beings which possess them. Hence it becomes necessary to view all Nature as an assemblage of living beings; and, once this is done, difficulties vanish and we can present a rational explanation of the universe and of life and evolution.

The idea of evolution has been held by philosophers from the earliest times, and is an alternative to the idea of special creation by the divine word. The idea that God created the universe at once, at some particular time in the past, is very unsatisfactory to thinking minds. It is natural to think, as we see everything changing and growing around us, that the whole universe and all that is in it has come into being by the same process of growth. The controversy between those who believe in special creation and those who believe in evolution was well illustrated some years ago by the celebrated case at Dayton, Tennessee, in which a young school teacher was tried for teaching his children the modern scientific doctrine of evolution. Most people probably thought the attitude taken up by the prosecution was very backward and narrow-minded, and that they showed little knowledge and less respect for the work of science. But yet one feels that they had some reason on their side. Crude as their reasoning may have been, they felt strongly that important issues turned on this question between the evolutionists and the religionists. The issue has been vividly and epigrammatically put in the phrase: 'Angel or Ape': did man descend from the angels or from the apes? In other words, it was felt that the evolutionists stood for a materialistic and animalistic view of human nature, as opposed to a spiritual and divine idea championed by their opponents. So it is hardly fair to accuse the religionists in this trial with making such a fuss merely about their Bible teachings, for there was more behind their zeal than that. They were championed by no less a person than W. J. Bryan, surely a man of intelligence and culture. It was the conviction that the scientific theories stood for materialism, animalism, a mechanical, mindless, soulless, godless universe; it was this feeling that actuated them and that still actuates many in their opposition. We may recall the bitter animosity aroused at the time when the modern scientific theory of biological evolution was first promulgated.

But at the same time we feel that the scientific side is worthy of our deep respect. It is represented by men of intelligence and worth, whose findings cannot be dismissed in such a wholesale way. It is owing to this that so many earnest thinkers have sought to find some way of reconciling the conflicting claims. It has been said, for instance, that, though God created the universe, he did not create it complete as it is now, but left it to evolve; that God is still creating the universe, his work being continual. It has been said that evolution represents the divine method or process. These are steps towards a unification of knowledge, but the matter needs to be much farther thrashed out. It is evident that the views of both sides in the controversy are very partial, containing truth mixed with error. The view which we stated above — that the universe consists of living beings — will enable us to solve the question.

II

THE MODERN SCIENTIFIC DOCTRINE OF EVOLUTION

IN the words of Huxley: "Evolution, or development, is in fact, at present employed in biology as a general name for the history of the steps by which any living being has acquired the morphological and the physiological characters which distinguish it." It is the theory that the various types of animals and plants have developed by descent with modification from other pre-existing types; and man is included in the animal kingdom and regarded as having been developed in this way from lower types in the animal kingdom. The general direction of this evolution has been from simpler types towards more complex and more highly organized types; but sometimes a retrograde movement has been observed. The attempt is to be able to trace the chain of evolving types back to a few very simple forms, or back even to a unicellular organism. Prominent among the names associated with these ideas comes the name of Lamarck, who held that the modifications occurring in organisms, and thus leading to their evolution, were brought about by response to their environment. This theory was developed by Darwin, and what is known as Darwinism has been defined as the theory which maintains that organisms tend to produce offspring varying slightly from their parents, and that the process of *natural selection* tends to favor the survival of individuals whose peculiarities render them best adapted to their surroundings. This is the doctrine of the *survival of the fittest*.

This means then that the higher types of organisms have been developed from lower types by the slow accumulation of small changes; that these small changes have been communicated from parent to offspring by procreation; that these small changes were caused by the effect of the environment (climate, food, enemies, etc.) upon the organism, causing it to change itself so as to become better adapted to its surroundings; that some of the changes thus produced did not survive, and only those best adapted to meet the conditions of life did survive; so that on the whole the trend of evolution was upwards towards more and more perfect forms. The theory does not give us any idea of the cause behind this process of evolution, nor of its purpose, nor its goal. It shows us a mechanical process going on, started we know not how or by whom, and reaching out towards an unknown destiny. In short it represents life as a mechanical process, devoid of soul and mind, end or purpose; and this is what causes the repugnance which many feel towards it.

Much study has been given to the subject since Darwin's time, and many of his views called in question; but the general theory of evolution is still held. Less importance is now attached to natural selection as a factor in evolution; indeed it is seen better than it was at first that natural selection is really a name for an effect; certain unspecified or unknown causes result in a natural selection; it is illogical therefore to speak of this result as if it were a cause.

The declared scientific method is to frame provisional hypotheses for the explanation of certain observed facts, and to change these hypotheses from time to time, as new facts are discovered. But the human mind has a tendency to fixed dogmas, and retains its provisional hypotheses too long; and when new facts are discovered which do not square with the hypotheses, will try to twist and force the evidence so as to make it square, rather than give up the theory. The scientific view of evolution has been gradually giving ground by sheer force of evidence, so that it becomes everyday more and more like what Theosophy teaches. This is an instance of the effects of candid and patient research in dispelling the dogmatic tendency.

The analogies between different types of organisms give a strong presumption that there has been evolution, but the difficulty has always been to find evidence of the actual process taking place. If the Darwinian theory is true, we ought to find intermediate forms between the existing forms and representing transition stages from one to another. But what we actually find is separate forms with gaps between. This however is explained by saying that the intermediate forms have disappeared as not being adapted to their environment; and it is pointed out that the palaeontological record supplies us with many such intermediate forms, which must have existed in long past ages when the conditions were different, but have since become extinct. But palaeontology shows us that the reptilia reached an acme of development in the Secondary Age, being represented by gigantic saurians, which now exist only as lizards a few inches long. So here we have an instance of a type reaching its fullest development and then dying out. This is one evidence that the plan of evolution is not so simple as was at first supposed; and it is but reasonable to suppose that the workings of Nature would be far more complex than any simple plan that might at first be thought of.

The later studies of biologists have confirmed the view that evolution, as it proceeds on the physical plane, tends rather to diversity than to uniformity; that each species tends to develop along its own special lines, and to diverge from the main trunk, rather than to lead on in a straight line to the next higher form in the scale. Moreover it has been found that species which have been differen-

tiated by external conditions, such as domest-
ication, tend to revert to their original type
when these special circumstances have been
removed. For instance, there is a type of fowl
called the jungle fowl, which seems to be the
original from which our numerous breeds of
fowls have come; and domestic fowls, if
turned wild, instead of preserving their acquired characteristics, soon revert to the primitive type of the jungle fowl. And the same
with other instances that are cited. This seems
to show that the evolution of types is not in
a straight line of continual progression from
simple to complex, but that each form tends
to diverge along its own special path. In fact
evolution has been compared to a tree, with
main trunk, limbs, branches, and twigs. The
species represent the branches and twigs;
while the main limbs are the primitive forms
from which they have diverged. If two forms
are found to be similar in structure, is this
evidence that one of them has been derived
from the other, or that both of them have
been derived from a common ancestor, each
then pursuing its own course, so that as time
goes on they get farther apart? In this latter
view, the multiplicity of forms which we see
today would seem to have diverged from a
comparatively few original forms.

Again, it is not clear that changes in species
are produced by hereditary transmission. The
elaborate studies which have been made in
genetics serve to complicate rather than to

solve the problem. But if small chance modifications are not transmitted by heredity, the general theory breaks down. And yet we can scarcely avoid the idea that there has been evolution, for such growth and development is evidently a general law of Nature. How escape from the dilemma?

These and many other difficulties which arise in the interpretation of evolution are due to the attempt to represent it as a purely physical process, and as a mechanical process; but with every succeeding day science is approaching nearer to a just view of the question. Biologists now give more importance to the organism itself than to its environment; and certainly no environment could produce any effect unless the organism itself responded to the influence. So that, if the effect of environment is alleged, it is necessary to *assume* that the individual is capable of responding to it; and this, to an unprejudiced mind, is tantamount to admitting that the individual is a living being, a being with some degree of feeling and intelligence — in fact a soul. Such a conclusion can only be avoided by falling back on 'inherent properties of matter,' or inherent properties of living matter, protoplasm; which is a very lame explanation, and is really no explanation at all. And the distinction between living matter and dead matter so-called, though admittedly a difference in kind, can hardly be an essential difference; for, if so, we should be obliged to suppose two kinds of matter in the universe, one living and the other not; an unnecessary complication, and one that leads to insuperable difficulties.

We observe in the mineral kingdom of so-called dead matter all kinds of wonderful properties and activities, which an unprejudiced mind might be disposed to regard as evidences of life and mind. But scientists, having assumed that this matter is dead, have been obliged to account for its properties and its activities by supposing the existence of blind 'forces,' the well-known physical forces of heat, light, electricity, magnetism, attraction and repulsion, cohesion, etc. And when asked to define these forces they define them by their effects, which is reasoning in a circle. If attraction is the coming together of two bodies, then it cannot be the cause which brings them together; that would be like saying that things are moved by motion. Heat is known to physics as something which is accompanied by molecular vibration, expansion, and other effects; but what it is that causes these effects remains a mystery; and the old explanation of an invisible agent is much more satisfactory. The forces which move matter so as to produce effects of heat, chemical action, etc., cannot be themselves material; or at least they must be of a finer kind of matter.

There seems no valid reason for admitting life in the plant and denying it to the mineral, though of course it must be conceded that life manifests itself in different ways in the different kingdoms of Nature. And thus we get back to the proposition that all Nature is composed of living beings, many of them microscopic in size, yet each of them organized, and each of them evolving and growing. With this proposition as a starting point, the doctrine of evolution becomes much easier to understand. We have more than once used the expression 'an unprejudiced mind'; and this refers to the fact that modern biologists, despite their professed freedom from religious bias, have nevertheless certain unconscious prejudices derived from the dogmatism of past generations. The theological notion of a God, outside the universe, who has created the universe, has given rise to the notion that there must have been a lot of dead matter which he used as material, or to which he has given life. So the notion of dead matter is a corollary to the notion of a God separate from his universe. We find that in antiquity people believed in the universal sentience of Nature, and that they still do so in parts where the idea of the theological God has not penetrated. People call this superstition and say that these ancients endowed dead things with imaginary life; whereas it is we who have invented the superstition that there are any dead things in Nature.

But of course what troubles people most in the controversy is the question of the origin of man. The idea that man has descended from an ape or any other animal is abhorrent. In order to avoid such a conclusion the anti-evolutionists have thought themselves obligated to deny much that science has affirmed to be fact. Hence they have put themselves into strange positions, hard to defend. But is there any such necessity of overthrowing science and denying things that cannot be denied? There is not. For, as has been shown, evolution cannot go on at all unless there are living beings who evolve, and the whole process is inconceivable except as a result of intelligence at work behind the scenes. This leads our thoughts to the true conception of evolution — spirit seeking to express itself in matter, soul embodying itself, mind creating for itself organs. Science has concentrated its gaze on the building and the building process, overlooking the builders and the plan. It has imagined a primordial germ, endowed with mysterious and undefined powers of growth, and developing itself through innumerable stages towards an unknown goal; feeling out experimentally into the infinite, as it were, and producing forms by a casual process of adaptation to surroundings. But biologists are more reasonable than they were in the days when H. P. Blavatsky criticized the evolutionary theories in her *Secret Doctrine;* and some of them admit now that the real agent in evolution is the animal itself. But to include forms below the animal kingdom, we must use a more general term and say that the agent is the *monad,* which means the living soul within the organism, whether that organism be animal, vegetable, or even mineral.

So evolution is a process of self-realization or manifestation carried on by the Cosmic Life or Spirit or Intelligence; God unfolding and revealing himself, we might say in theological language; and Nature the visible garb of Deity. Evolution must be considered as a twofold process — spirit involving into matter, and matter evolving after the pattern of spirit. These two are often called involution and evolution, but the one word evolution is as often applied to the whole process. Such variations in the use of words have to be recognized and allowed for. But the point here is that mind has not evolved upwards as matter has. It has involved down into matter. So the attempt to imagine an evolution of mind parallel with the evolution of form in the kingdoms of nature is wrong and creates confusion. This confusion culminates in the attempt to argue that the intelligence of man has evolved from the intelligence of beasts. There is a radical difference between the mind of man and that of even the highest beast: *self-consciousness; this is either present or absent and does not come in stages.*

Evolution means the unfolding of what is latent, and thus implies that the original germ contains in potentiality all that is afterwards manifested. Evolution does not mean a putting together of separate parts so as to make a composite; it is not an additive process. Such a method would make a building or a machine, not an organism; or rather it would not even make that, for the building and machine must pre-exist as a plan in the mind of the designer. It is true that the seed draws to itself elements from soil and air to build its structure; but the building is done according to a model. Before the plant exists as a physical organism visible to the eye, it has already existed as an astral organism, and could be seen as such by the eye of a clairvoyant. And when the plant decays, that astral organism remains, to form the model for future physical organisms of the same kind.

At the time of writing we continually come across utterances by leading biologists, which show an increasing readiness to accept the views here indicated. They see more clearly now that a mere description of *process* is not a sufficient explanation of evolution, and that there is no escape from the conclusion that intelligent forces are behind the process. Nay, even the physicists are saying the same thing, and are in some ways more reasonable than the biologists. They see that their 'forces' are merely effects produced in matter by the agency of something unknown; and they have analyzed matter to a point whence it is impossible to proceed further without passing the bounds of matter. However complete may be the physical explanation of natural phenomena, it is complete only within the limits assigned; and still leaves plenty of scope for the introduction of ultra-physical agencies without in the least upsetting the physical explanation. And some physicists have taken the inevitable step and cut the knot by inferring that even physical matter is actuated by living forces — that is, by living beings.

III

THE ASTRAL PLANE

EVOLUTIONISTS, in their attempts to interpret the evolutionary process, are much hampered by a neglect to take into account the existence of other kinds of matter than the familiar physical matter. But, as explained in Manual No. 10 on THE ASTRAL LIGHT, it is impossible to explain the phenomena of physical matter without assuming the existence of a subtler form of matter behind these phenomena. As said above, a growing plant seems to build itself up mysteriously, according to its peculiar pattern, without visible agency to account for such building. The explanation is that the entire form of the plant exists beforehand in astral matter, and that upon this model is built the physical structure, the physical atoms taking their places in accordance therewith. In the scale of plants and animals, the changes take place in the astral form of the organism, not in the physical structure; and thus is explained the gaps in the chain. This has been illustrated by the following analogy: If people are ascending a spiral staircase, a spectator looking from one side will see people at different

stages, but will not see how they pass from
one stage to the next. He may assume that
they jump, or that they proceed by gradual
ascent; but he will fail to see the process actually at work. The fact is that the people
pass by gradual ascent round the back parts
of the spiral, which are hidden from view.
The physical species on earth remain un-
altered for long periods; but this does not
mean that there is no evolution. These physical forms are merely the successive houses
in which the evolving *monad* dwells; but the
monad itself is evolving all the time; its evolutionary changes take place in the astral form,
and when thus changed it incarnates in the
corresponding physical form.

At this point it is advisable to consider what
we really mean by an animal or a vegetable.
The asumption that it is merely a physical
organism is wrong, and we cannot explain
evolution on such a wrong assumption. The
plant or animal is essentially a *monad* — a
living soul, a spark of the cosmic Fire, an
atom of the universal Mind and Life and
Spirit. It is performing a pilgrimage through
Matter, in the course of which it is gradually
and progressively evolving various forms for
the expression of its own latent capacities.
It is a growing learning thing. This monad is
a seed, and contains within itself all the potentialities of its divine origin. This monad
or spark of life is imbodied; but not merely
in a physical body, for beyond the physical

there are other imbodiments in subtler forms of matter. It has a psycho-mental imbodiment, which makes of it an animal (or a plant) soul; this again has an astral imbodiment, and this again a physical imbodiment. All this has to be considered if evolution is to be rightly understood.

If we would look within our own consciousness, we should get a clearer idea than by looking at the outside of things. We find that we are primarily a self-conscious thinking being; our organs and bodies are instruments which we have built for ourselves in order to express ourselves in and to contact the outer world. We grow from within. It is the same everywhere; everything is growing, and everything grows from within. Visible plants and animals come out of the invisible; and it is in the invisible that the evolutionary changes take place. As the soul of the being gradually develops, the changes in it are produced in the astral form, and thence transferred to the physical form.

Again, as is said in the Manual on THE ASTRAL LIGHT, it is impossible to explain how the body of a plant or animal could remain the same throughout life when the physical atoms are continually changing, unless there is some permanent mold upon which those physical atoms are built and which preserves the integrity of the organism through all the changes of its physical atoms.

Thus we cannot explain evolution without

taking into account the existence of the astral plane and the astral bodies of organisms. But, once this is grasped, the difficulty disappears.

IV

THE EVOLUTION OF MAN
The Meaning of the Word 'Man'

WE must first know what we are to understand by the word 'man.' If we may for the purposes of the argument assume (though without admitting) that the scientific evolutionists are right in their theories as to the evolution of the human body, we should still be left entirely in the dark as to the origin of the human intelligence, the human soul — in a word, of man himself. This is what the anti-evolutionists feel so strongly, however inadequately they may be able to express their objections. They feel that the acceptance of the scientific view would commit them to an animalistic materialistic and brutalizing conception of human nature. It is true that scientists may reply that they are not concerned with this aspect of the question, they only study physical facts. Yet the fact remains that such a materialistic and mechanistic view does actually influence our minds and tend to promote in us a pessimistic view of human nature. In other words, science tends to become a religion, and a religion which denies Deity, or at least disregards Deity; a religion which emphasizes the brutish instincts in man; a religion which accustoms us to look back to the animal world for our ancestry. Not even the animal mind, nay not the intelligence that makes the plant grow true to kind and perform its functions, can be interpreted as mechanical or chemical products. Still less, very much less, the mind of man. Let us look within and try to sound the depths of our marvelous conscious being. If that came from matter, then matter must be God. Like creates like, and streams cannot flow higher than their source. Our consciousness is part of an ocean of consciousness; our mind is a little focus of light; and our organism cannot furnish more than the screen upon which the light falls.

Theosophy deals with facts, and what fact can be more factual than our own conscious existence? We cannot find anything more fundamental than our own consciousness to use as a starting point. The evolution of spirit is in the opposite direction to that of matter; by the conjunction of the two is formed mind. Man is (broadly speaking) the result of two lines of evolution coalescing: that of spirit from above, and that of matter from below. The whole manifested universe is created by the union of spirit and matter, by the cosmic life and intelligence building for itself vehicles for its expression. As said before, it may be better to speak of the involution of spirit into matter, and the consequent evolution of matter. Science has studied the evolution of matter, but not the involution of spirit. Moreover, it has sought to make both conform to the same process, and to represent mind as having evolved upward through the animate kingdoms to man. It is spirit which causes the organisms to evolve; the form changes and adapts itself to the growing capacities of the indwelling monad. If an analogy from science itself were asked, we might mention the case of heat entering a body and causing it to undergo many changes, as from water to steam, or any one of the innumerable chemical changes produced by heat. We see here that the heat is the invisible agent which promotes the visible changes. But biologists have argued as if the changes took place of themselves, and the heat were a by-product of the process. If it is necessary for a devotee of science to shut off all his finer sensibilities and to view nature with a cold eye, he might fail to see in the eye of the animal that spark of conscious light which he might recognize as akin with his own; otherwise he might see the animal as a thing in itself, apart from its mere body.

Self-conscious Mind

But to speak of man particularly — he is not the end product of the chain of plant and animal forms; for there is a very marked gap, the gap of self-consciousness, as said above. Man has the power to study his own con-

sciousness, and he has the power to alter himself by an act of will and imagination. These
faculties the animals have not; and these
faculties are either wholly present or wholly
absent; they do not exist in any intermediate
or partial stages. Here it is necessary to am-
plify a statement which was made in a qual-
ified manner above, when we said that man
is a product of a twofold evolution. We will
consider him now as a product of *three* distinct
lines of evolution. The third line is the line of
the self-conscious mind.

As said in religious cosmogonies, our Bible
included, man was created in the first instance
out of the dust of the ground, and made a
living soul — that is (according to a more
exact rendering of the Hebrew) an animal
soul. Later, this soul was endowed with the
divine fire, so that man was created in the
divine likeness. This is a universal tenet;
nothing has ever been more a matter of
agreement than that of the double creation of
man. It is a truth, and we shall witness its
confirmation by science, though science may
use terms of its own instead of the Biblical
phraseology.

By observing facts we shall find that intelligence is communicated from mind to mind,
or, to speak more accurately, it is aroused in
one mind by the action of another. A child,
left to itself, would not develop or evolve intelligence, but would remain a sort of instinctual creature, as has actually happened

in some recorded cases. But he learns from his parents and growing family, both by instruction and imitation; and is afterwards taught in schools. Great movements in thought have always been started by master minds, thinkers of force and originality, who have gathered round them disciples, and thence the wave of thought has spread through the mass. Light is always handed on. It is true that intelligence lies latent in every man, but it would continue to lie latent unless called into manifestation. The highest types of animals remain what they are, and show no tendency to develop intelligence. What reason can be alleged for supposing that it was anywise different in some past age? The hope of finding the fossil remains of creatures intermediate between man and the higher apes has not been successful; and it is likely that the bones of degenerate human types would be mistaken for such links. The analogy between the structure of anthropoid and man works both ways, and may equally well prove the descent of the ape from the man; and there are biologists who believe that the evidence is in favor of that view.

Man is, then, the product of *three* principal lines of evolution, the third line being the *Mânasic* evolution — that is, the evolution of *Manas,* which means self-conscious mind. It is this self-conscious mind which so sharply distinguishes man from the animal species; and, as said before, it cannot be represented as a product of direct evolution from the un-self-conscious mind which animals have. It was a distinct acquisition made by man at a particular stage of his evolution. There was a time when he had it not; there was a time when he gained it. This marks the difference between the early 'mindless' Races of humanity and the later 'awakened' races.

This event is called in Theosophy the Coming of the *Mânasaputras,* which means 'Sons of Mind.' These were godlike beings who had once been men; but, as they belonged to a previous Round of the evolutionary cycle, they had evolved beyond the status of humanity as known today. It is from these beings that man derived his special intelligence. But it must not be thought that they *gave* him mind, as one gives a gift to someone who has it not. What they did was to awaken in the mindless man the latent seed of self-conscious mind which was already in him. For we must bear in mind that the highest potentialities lie dormant in every being in the universe, however lowly, awaiting development into active power at some time in the future, however remote. The Sons of Mind, then, were the Teachers or Instructors of man, the Awakeners or Saviors. This event is described in allegorical language in many sacred scriptures and mythologies, our own Biblical *Genesis* included. The Manual on MAN'S DIVINE PARENTAGE AND DESTINY: *The Great Rounds and Races* speaks more fully of this branch of the subject, and to this we must refer the reader for further information.

In the present place we must limit ourselves to what is necessary to explain the present topic. It is this mânasic part of man which forms the necessary link between Spirit and Matter. We have to imagine a natural evolution proceeding from below, and producing more and more complex forms, and a Spiritual evolution (more properly involution) descending from above. But the Spiritual Beings are unable to incarnate in the animal organisms produced by the lower evolution, the gap being too great; so that it is this intermediate principle, Manas or self-conscious mind, intelligence, which bridges the gap, bringing the Spiritual into union with the physical, and thus making the complete man.

Our own familiar experience will give us illustration of the fact that such is the method by which knowledge is actually conveyed from one person to another. We all learn from contact with other minds. These minds do not *give* us something, but rather arouse our our latent capacities. This is the true meaning of education, which means 'drawing forth,' as shown by Plato in the well-known story where he *elicits* geometrical truth from an untaught slave.

If it is asked whether the present animals will ever become men, the answer, as we said above, is Yes and No. It is not true to say

that beast bodies can evolve into human bodies, or that animals become men by gradual
transformation. But it is true that the Monads
now inhabiting animal bodies will one day
pass over into the human kingdom and become enlightened with the fire of mind. But
this will not occur in the present Round; the
door into the human kingdom is now closed
for this Round, and the present beasts await
their turn in a future Round.

LIMITED VIEW OF SCIENCE

It has been well said that physical science
is of a highly metaphysical nature, and this
is obviously true of the evolutionist philosophy.
Those who uphold it seem hypnotized with
the idea that things are developing upwards
from the very simplest beginnings; but what
a view of the world scheme does this make in
our minds! The amount of things which we
must presuppose and take for granted is
wonderful. Upon the atom and its innate
properties are loaded the whole responsibility
of the universe and all its beings. Well may
we call it the Almighty Atom! But, apart
from this, the movement from simplicity to
complexity is only one half of an observable
universal process, the other being the movement from complexity to simplicity; and these
two processes are working both at once and
all the time. The processes at work in cosmic
evolution are vast and various, and the whole

scheme is infinitely elaborate and complicated. Science has hold of an important truth, but has glimpsed only a small part of its workings; the hypotheses of science are timid and confined. Again, science is unconsciously affected by the shortened view of human history fostered by religious teaching; and consequently seems determined to allow man only a few short years at the end of its time scale. This shortened idea of human history is further favored by the determination to make man the latest product of an end-on evolution.

Archaeology is continually frustrating these attempts, and is always bringing to light new evidence that man, even highly civilized man, is of vast antiquity. An examination of the facts, without the pre-existing prejudice, would have led us to different conclusions; for in truth there is nothing to show that man has recently developed up from savagery.

And in biology too it has to be admitted that the structure of the human body shows a primitivenes which ill accords with the view that it is the most recent product of evolution. Man is in fact the original and therefore the most primitive stock of all, and bears in his body primitive arrangements of bones and muscles. As scientific authority for this statement may be called for, we refer to MAN IN EVOLUTION, by G. de Purucker, pp. 124-26, and following, where are enumerated at length a number of anatomical details in confirmation, chiefly drawn from the anatomist

Dr. Wood-Jones. A synopsis of them is given in the Appendix of this Manual.

MAN THE MOST PRIMITIVE STOCK

According to the real teachings as to evolution, as given by Theosophy, and speaking for the present only of evolution in this Fourth Round, man was actually the original and root stock of the mammalians, and the other stocks have sprung from the human stem. This accounts for these primitive and simple conformations in the human body. In the various animal stocks we find specializations of particular organs and functions, such as wings, trunks, claws, horns, gills. These, according to the theory which evolutionists have been trying to establish, are features which have been discarded; but their presence is much more consistent with the Theosophical doctrine of evolution than with the theory of the evolutionists. According to the Theosophical doctrine, the human stem threw off from itself the germs of the future animal stocks, and these germs then proceeded to develop and specialize, each along its own peculiar line, so that as time went on the tendency was towards ever wider divergence. And a candid study of the facts shows that this is the case; for it is found that species do actually tend to specialize along their own lines, rather than to pass by gradation into other species.

In saying that the germs which afterwards

developed into the mammals were thrown off from the human stem, it is necessary to add a qualification and to explain why we said 'human stem' rather than 'man.' The events referred to took place in the very far past, and since then the human race has been developing, so that the humanity from which the mammals were thrown off was very different from the humanity of today. It is also necessary to bear in mind that, in a universe where everything evolves, matter itself has been evolving; and that its present stage, which we call 'physical' represents the latest phase of a continuous succession of phases or states through which matter has passed. The process by which the germs or seeds which were afterwards to evolve into the mammalian stocks were thrown off is one that biologists call 'budding' or 'gemmation.' The present human organism is not able to produce offspring in this way, though this method of reproduction exists today in some of the lower orders of creatures.

So the question, Did the animals descend from man? can be answered both by Yes and No; they did descend in the way described here, but not in the Darwinian sense. They did not come from men by procreation and as the end product of a single line upward evolution; the germs of the animal stocks did proceed from the human stock, at a time in the far past when that human stock was not like what it is now. Thus the type of evolution in the animate kingdoms is like a tree with a main trunk, branch trunks, boughs, twigs, and leaves. This is quite different from the single-line type of evolution at first imagined, and science itself is coming more and more to this tree-like form of evolution, as facts accumulate and as studies progress.

Man Descends from — Man

The ancestors of man were — man himself; prehuman perhaps, but still man. And this necessitates that something be said as to what man is and whence he has come.

Man came into existence on the spiritual plane as an un-self-conscious spark of divinity, destined, after cycles of evolution, to return to unity with the divine essence from whence he sprang. He is a monad, a germ of the Universal Life. The monads destined to become men were thus godlike beings who came to earth in the earliest days of the planet's life. The first *physical* man existed on this earth 18,000,000 years ago; but before that, man existed on earth in astral or ethereal form. Here is a point which the modern theories have overlooked — that matter itself evolves, and that the earth was not always physical. This has a great bearing on the whole picture of palaeontology, and many difficulties arise from supposing that the conditions and properties of matter were the same in very remote periods as they are now.

In the present Globe-Round of cosmic evolution there are seven human Root-Races, of which we are now in the Fifth. The First Root-Race was in Palaeozoic times. Each of these Races had its own peculiar form and its peculiar method of reproduction, the First by fission, the Second by budding, the Third by androgynous generation and egg-laying. These methods are still found in some kinds of animals. The present method of sexual reproduction is a passing phase. The progenitors of the mammalian stocks were the first physical men and the astral-ethereal men who preceded them. At this time man was 'mindless' — that is, he was instinctual, for the light of self-consciousness had not yet been kindled in him. He was able at that time to start the evolution of the various mammalian types by the cells or seeds cast off from his own body. These then pursued each its own special line of evolution, thus during the ages producing those widely divergent types which we see today.

Thus far we have spoken of the mammalia; there remain the types below, namely reptiles, bird, fishes, etc. These did not issue from the human stem in this Globe-Round of the great evolutionary cycle, but in a preceding Globe-Round. It is thus seen that the plan of evolution is much more complex than has been supposed. We do not propose to go into it here more fully or in more detail; and this may cause what is said to appear scrappy; but the plan is fully elaborated in other Theosophical writings, and its consistency can there be seen.

MAN AND THE APES

A special case has to be noted as regards the two classes of simians, the anthropoids and the monkeys. As surmised by many men of science, these are *from* man and not toward him. But they differ from the other mammals in the way in which they were derived from the human stem. The early Race of mankind spoken of above as being 'mindless' allied themselves with certain of the animals existing at that time, and from this union sprang a hybrid race which is the ancestry of the present monkeys (as distinguished from anthropoid apes). It is not right to call this miscegenation a crime, as such an act would be regarded today, because neither the humans nor the animals concerned in it were like the humans and animals of today. They were much more like each other; the distance between human and animal was not so great. Hence a fertile union was possible, and also a fertile offspring able to perpetuate its own race. Moreover, the humans being mindless were incapable of sin, and their acts were instinctual. This took place during the Mesozoic Age.

As to the manlike apes, their history is as follows. At a later date, during the Miocene period, when the Fourth great Race of humanity has passed its climax, certain degenerate remnants thereof repeated the act of the 'mindless' (as just mentioned), by allying themselves with the then existing simian stock; and thus sprang the anthropoid apes. This act was, however, one of bestiality, a sin, because these humans were not mindless but endowed with self-consciousness. It is still to be observed, however, that human and animals were even then not far enough apart to prevent a fertile and self-reproductive union. Neither man nor monkey were the same as now, both having since evolved along their respective lines.

Such is the story of the origin of the apes and monkeys; and proofs of its truth are to be found in a study of the anatomical features of man and the anthropoids, which will be seen to confirm the above teaching rather than the view that man has developed from the ape, or that both have developed from a common animal stock.

SPIRITUAL URGE IN EVOLUTION

It is clear then that we can accept evolution without disparaging the nature of man; all we need to do is to get the doctrine straight and complete, not twisted and partial. It is materialism, not evolution, that denies the divinity of man. Man is not his body; the latter may be a product of evolution from below, but man himself is a self-conscious being, with infinite untapped resources within him. It is this infinite part which has come from above; this is the fire which has kindled in the animal body the fire of genius.

We stated that, in one sense, man is from the animals; which means that the body which man has is the result of ages of evolution through lower kingdoms. But such evolution upward could never have been accomplished without a simultaneous involution of spirit into matter from above. It is the universal Life, Consciousness, Spirit (an exact term is hard to find), which is the cause of evolution, in seeking to build for itself new and better mansions on earth. But Life, Consciousness, and Spirit are mere abstractions in themselves; they are the attributes of living beings, and these living beings are the Monads, of various classes and degrees.

Monads are sparks or atoms of the universal Life; they are spiritual beings, and may be regarded as the ultimate seed or germ of every living thing, down to the smallest atom or particle. Each of these germs starts its own line of evolution; in it lie stored up and latent the potentiality of all that will develop from it. Thus the whole universe is the scene of a host of such living evolving beings. They are at varying stages of their evolution; when spirit first begins to involve itself in matter, the evolution is very slow; so that long ages are passed in the lower kingdoms of nature — the mineral, and before that the three elemental kingdoms, then the vegetable, and so on.

' Individualization begins in the plants, develops farther in the animals, and is completed in man. But observe, it is not the organic forms that change one into another, but the indwelling monads, which inhabit one form after another, as their evolution requires. Thus the forms may remain stationary or nearly so for long periods, while all the time evolution is proceeding.

EVOLUTIONARY WAVES

It is interesting to note here that some scientists have noticed that new varieties of plants and animals appear *suddenly;* this is in response to a particular urge from within, requiring the production of that kind of a body for the expression of what is within the monad.

All this has an important bearing on past evolution, as recorded in the palaeontological record, and clears up many puzzles which that record has presented. While it is true on the whole that the types get lowlier as we recede into the past, yet the development has been by no means uniform. There have been great bursts of some particular type, like that of the reptiles in the Mesozoic Age, which attained such enormous development and gigantic size, and has dwindled until the little sun lizard represent the once gigantic saurian. At one

time there was an inmmense development of
tree-ferns, at another of ammonites, and so on.
Concurrently with this evolution of the plants
and animals there were changes in the structure of the earth, the distribution of land and
water, the nature of the atmosphere, the tem-
perature and pressure, and other geophysical
conditions; all of which makes the plan of
evolution much more variegated than that of
simple lineal descent.

Theosophy agrees with Darwinism in the
belief that there is a law of gradual and extremely slow evolution embracing many mil-
lion years. But it is necessary to distinguish
between the fact of evolution and the manner
of it; and in this latter point Theosophy may
find itself in disagreement. And yet again
there is the question of the cause of evolution,
another moot question subject to diverse
opinions.

One evolutionist is quoted as holding that
evolution is accomplished by the agency of
the 'energies which are intrinsic in the evolving matter, and without interference from
agencies external to matter.' Here we find
a good example of the method of evading a
prime difficulty by the use of an undefined
word — in this case 'intrinsic' — which really begs the whole question to be solved. The
word was probably used to exclude the action
of a divine creator and thus to distinguish the
evolutionary theory from that of special creation. But it really replaces one difficulty by

another of equal or greater magnitude. In the first place it might prove hard to distinguish between intrinsic and extrinsic, to say just what is within matter and what is without. Is an 'agency intrinsic in matter' itself material? If this agency is itself material, then we have not solved the problem but merely moved it one stage farther. If the said intrinsic energy is not material, then what is it? The whole materialistic theory seems to be given away at once. Again, if the energy is not material, but is immaterial and separate from matter, then what becomes of the difference between intrinsic and extrinsic? The author of the above remark, however, goes on to say that intrinsic energies are a 'property of the physical basis of tridimensional matter.' This seems to imply that there can be something beyond matter, something which is not tridimensional; but the idea is spoilt by calling it 'physical.' It is evident, on any logical reasoning, that matter is either actuated by some agency which is not material (or not material in the same sense), or else this matter is the *primum mobile*, the primary element, the self-created or uncreated ultimate cause of all things — in a word, God.

Logically speaking, mind is prior to matter; for all we can know of matter is what we find in our own mind. That is, we must *assume* mind before the question can be argued at all. The result of defying this fundamental rule of logic is the hopeless confusion described above. There seem to have been people actually capable of arguing that consciousness has been evolved from a matter which did not already possess it. Anything from which the human mind has evolved must be greater than that mind, whether we call it matter or an atom or a monad or a God. In this sense it may be true to say that evolution is caused by the powers intrinsic in matter; but this would then be only another way of saying that in every smallest atom there resides in potency the whole of whatever may afterwards be evolved from it. That is, this atom is a spark of the universal Spirit — which is pure Theosophical teaching.

V

THE ANTIQUITY OF MAN

THEOSOPHY has to hold the balance between religious dogmatism and scientific dogmatism, and between materialism in both camps. The scientific teachings as to evolution (or insofar at least as they have not corrected themselves in recent years) may lie open to the charge of promoting a derogatory view of human nature, as tending to concentrate our attention on the animal side of our nature, to the neglect of our spiritual endowments. But this charge has also been laid at the door of religion. In many of its forms it has encouraged the belief that man is by nature corrupt and born in sin; that he does not possess the power of saving himself, but needs a propitiatory sacrifice and the help of a church. Both these views are destructive to human interests, and the religious opponents of evolution would have better success against the materialism of their opponents if they stood on surer ground themselves. But there is nothing in evolution, rightly understood, to disparage the nature of man; on the contrary the faith of man in his own essential divinity and perfectibility is greatly increased. Neither science nor religion can be wrong in themselves, but materialism may creep into either of them.

In the Manual MAN'S DIVINE PARENTAGE AND DESTINY already referred to, we learn much that dovetails with what is said in the present Manual; so it is not necessary to repeat it at length. But something needs to be said about the antiquity of man on earth. Science seems unconsciously to have inherited a prejudice from religion to the effect that man is a recent product; and there can be little doubt that the scientific interpretation of the available evidence has been largely colored by this prejudice. The notion has been furthered by the crude idea of the evolutionary scale, which is represented as a single-track ascent from primitive forms up to the most complex; which requires that we shall regard the most complex as the most recent arrivals upon earth. The theory also requires that we shall find an evolution in civilization, that the man of today shall be the most civilized, and the most progressed intellectually and morally, while preceding peoples shall be less and less cultivated as we get back farther.

Unfortunately for this view, it has not been confirmed by facts; and with every day the evidence against it is accumulating. It is a feather in the cap of science that it hunts industriously for the facts in archaeology, thereby discovering things that confute its own theories; but it is not a feather in the cap when anyone tries to hide or distort the evidence to fit the theory; and both things happen. It has become a commonplace nowadays to say that we find ancient cultures, like that of of the Egyptian, already attained to a degree which presupposes an extremely long past behind them; or to point to the evident fact that civilizations decay as well as develop. In short, a candid study of the archaeological record gives no support to the idea that there has been any such upward development of civilization in recent times. As we go farther back we do not seem to get any nearer to a beginning. Civilizations seem to have arisen in the far past, gone through their phases, and passed away, to be succeeded by others, which have in turn gone through the stages of birth, growth, and dissolution.

The human stem is the main trunk from which other organic forms have at one time or another sprung. Such is the thesis of Theosophy, and this need not be accepted as a dogma, for the facts which come to light will tend ever more and more to confirm it. But though we may not swallow a doctrine on blind faith, but must always seek confirmation by our own judgment, still it helps very much and saves infinite time spent in wayward wandering, if we can have the key in our mind from the start. All teachers lay down their propositions in advance of the demonstrations, thus making reasonable demands on the confidence of their pupils, who are willing to accept statements provisionally until such time as they can be justified. Theosophists therefore feel no compuction in stating boldly their fundamental propositions.

The results of archaeology therefore tend rather in favor of the Theosophical doctrine of man's origin than in favor of the current theories. The evolution is cyclical rather than progresive in a straight line. The traces of peoples of a primitive type and culture, which are unearthed, differ not from the type and culture of peoples that exist on earth today; and side by side with these primitive types, in the past as in the present, dwelt mighty civilizations. Humanity is divided into races, and subdivided indefinitely into lesser divisions, and each one of these divisions is in some particular phase of its own racial evolution. Some are on the upgrade, some on the down; and so we find on earth today races that are rising, others that have passed their zenith, and some that are dying out. So it has been in the past; but the remnants of cultured peoples are more perishable than those of the uncultured. Even so, the attempt to find confirmation of the theories has not met with success. Nor is there satisfactory evidence that the type of the human organism has changed, except in minor details, and these fluctuating, since the earliest periods we can contact.

The whole story of cosmic evolution is too complex to be delineated here, and would only serve to confuse the reader even if we attempted it; so we will repeat what was said above — namely that in this *manvantara* there are seven great periods known as Globe-Rounds, of which we are at present in the fourth; and that in each Globe-Round there are seven Root-Races of humanity, of which we are now in the Fifth. It is millions of years ago since this Fifth Root-Race began, and the First Root-Race was coeval with the Palaeo-zoic Age in geology. It is 18,000,000 years since man first appeared on earth in physical form; but before that he existed on earth in finer forms of matter, sometimes called astral or ethereal. The time scale with which we have to deal is therefore large; but this should raise no objection when we consider the vast ages demanded by the palaeontologists, the geologists, and the astronomers.

Many people must have been struck by the disparity between these vast periods and the shortness of history as usually visioned. A similar remark applies to the vastness of the spatial scale contemplated in astronomy. In view of this it would seem that Theosophy is merely introducing proportion where before there was disproportion. These Root-Races are subdivided into smaller divisions, and these again into yet smaller, so that the racial cultures at present on earth represent very small offshoots. Further, as every racial division splits up and gives rise to branches, each pursuing it s own separate history, it can be seen that what we find now on earth is a very miscellaneous assortment, some of them being remote descendants of the Fourth Root-Race, and a few even of the Third. The mixture of racial remnants in Africa is very remarkable.

In view of this, what can we think of the timid attempts of historians and ethnologists to trace the origin of one little division of humanity from another, and to piece together a consistent picture out of such a scrap heap? The decaying remnants of some mighty race that flourished millions of years ago are represented as a primitive stock from which our present civilized humanity has evolved; and attempts are made to find still more lowly types leading back by gradations into the animal kingdom. The result is that theory after theory has to be given up as new facts come to light. Another important point is that much is lost by studying things piece-meal and in departmentalizing science too much. One result of this is that one branch of science may devise theories which do not suit other branches. But today expansion is taking place in all directions and the spirit of devotion to truth is bound to prevail over parochialism and obscurantism and to bring the facts to light.

VI

HEREDITY AND EVOLUTION

THE scientific study of evolution is interwoven with the study of genetics and with that of cytology. The former deals with the observed facts concerning heredity, as ascertained by statistical investigations into human heredity and experimental breeding with plants and animals; the latter means the study of cells, their functioning and their development. To go into details on these subjects would require volumes, but the leading points, in their bearing on our present topic, may be summarized. The story, historically considered, is one of theory succeeding theory; a drama which is itself an example of evolution, since it represents the growth of ideas under the modifying inflence of facts. Earlier theories, based on imperfect knowledge, have been successively changed, as new facts came to light; and it is a well-known circumstance in most investigations, that the new facts, instead of confirming the old theories and thus simplifying the inquiry, open out new vistas, so that the problem becomes more and more complex.

The main problems to be solved are:

(1) How do these investigations affect the theories of evolution? Do they support it or conflict with it? The general answer can be surmised: the investigations call for modifications of the theory, but it is still held to, so far as the facts will permit.

(2) To what extent does heredity tend towards permanence of type, and to what extent does it tend to produce variation? The general answer to this is that both phenomena coexist, and that there are certain factors within the cell which tend to pass on heredimaments from generation to generation, and certain other factors which tend to produce variations.

(3) To what extent are characters acquired by an individual transmissible to offspring? This question is closely involved with —

(4) Is variation due to the hereditary transmission of acquired characters, or is it produced within the germinal cell by some other means?

Let us consider the earlier views on evolution and ask what effect has been produced on them by later studies. The idea was that new varieties were produced from old by the slow accumulation of small variations, which were transmitted by heredity; and that this slow process, continued through ages, has resulted in a gradual progressive evolution from the simplest forms up to the most complex. This has been found to be too simple and crude a theory; and in this respect the work of Bateson of more than a half century ago may be regarded as of historical import- ance. He was president of the British Asso- ciation for the Advancement of Science, at its annual meeting for 1914, which was held at Toronto; and gave on that occasion a re- markable address from which we may quote. He makes a distinction between a connecting link and a mere mongrel. He instances the case of two allied species of plants, called *Lychnis diurna* and *Lychnis vespertina,* which are found in the same area, accompanied by many plants which show a number of varia- tions between the two. These used to be re- garded as transitional steps, but they are merely mongrels between the two species. He says:

Knowledge of heredity has so reacted on our concep- tions of variation that very competent men are even denying that variation in the old sense is a genuine occurrence at all. Variation is postulated as the basis of all evolutionary change. Do we then as a matter of fact find in the world about us variations occurring of such a kind as to warrant faith in a contemporary progressive evolution? Till lately, most of us would have answered 'Yes' without misgiving.

Variation is found wherever a number of varieties of the same species are crossing freely. But these variations are 'factorial' — that is, the various individuals possess in various rela- tive proportions certain constituents of the original breed from which they have all diverged. This is the same result as is produced by experimental breeding. The important point is that the varieties are not brought about by the addition of new factors but by the loss of certain factors, the totality of which factors were present in the original parent. He also considers the case of the numerous breeds of domestic fowls, all derived from an original 'jungle fowl.' These domestic fowls are not transition forms leading from one species to another, as the original theory would require; but they are factorial products of the original wild hen, each containing some of the factors present in that bird, and all containing the factors in varying proportions. In other words, the domestic breeds are divergent offshoots from the original type. To quote again:

We have no longer the smallest doubt in all these examples [domestic animals and various wild animals and plants] the varieties stand in a regular descending order, and that they are simple terms in a series of combinations of factors separately transmitted, of which each may be present or absent.

The name of De Vries is associated with the Mutation theory; he was led by his experiments in plant heredity to the conclusion that changes might take place much more suddenly than had been supposed. The earlier evolutionists had supposed that variations were slight and cumulative; but he found that from seedlings of the same plant may come individual plants differing from each other not only slightly but sometimes very radically; and in exceptional cases the deviation may be so marked that one of the plants may fairly be regarded as constituting a new species. Such a sudden variation De Vries called a mutation.

Weismann and his Germ-Plasm theory next calls for mention. His main idea still holds ground, though subsequent studies in cytology have modified the views of biologists as to details. He held that, in many-celled organisms, certain of the cells die as individual cells, and build up the structure and substance of the body, being concerned with nutrition and other vital functions; but that certain other cells do not thus die but perpetuate themselves by the method of fision, as occurs in single-cell organisms; and that these latter cells are handed on from generation to generation. This would account for the perpetuation of ancestral features throughout all generations, and explain why breeding takes place true to type. It leaves open the question whether these perpetual cells are or are not influenced by environmental influence, or whether any changes they may undergo originate from some cause within the cell itself. The deeper study of the cell under powerful microscopes has now resolved it into a number of genetic elements, the description of which belongs to the study of biology; and it is sufficient for present purposes to say that it is recognized that some of these elements are concerned with the building and nutrition of the body, and others are concerned with reproduction.

Professor Bateson in more recent utterances has said that to watch the marvelous actions of the cell and its constituents is like watching an act of creation at work; and others have said that there is nothing in the appearance of these elements which can give us the least idea of what they will do. And the polar structure observable at some stages, and the radiating lines like those proceeding from a magnet, suggest the presence of *electric* forces and point to the strong evidences of *purposive* action. It is thus that men of science are finding themselves forced by the facts ever nearer and nearer to the inevitable truth — that mere mechanism can explain nothing, but that life and living beings prevail throughout.* (See Appendix)

These studies in heredity and cytology, then, show us that changes of type are produced with comparative rareness and suddenness, and that as a general rule each type reproduces its own kind, subject to temporary variations produced by crossing and environ-

---

* The amazing advances of more recent years in biological study should also be closely followed and related to basic Theosophical views.

ment. This agrees with what was said above about the various types of organic beings having been produced originally from seeds thrown off by the human stock at a primitive stage in the evolution of the latter. Each of these seeds, thus thrown off, then proceeds to follow its own independent evolution, true to its own particular type. But within every one of these evolving organisms there dwells the 'monad,' or animal or genetable soul, so to speak. It is all the while developing and garnering experience from its contact with the outer world. By this means it gradually gains new capacities; but these lie latent and unexpressed, until such time as outer circumstances may permit them to find expression. And then there takes place one of these 'mutations' or sudden variations. This is the invisible cause which brings them about. Thus too it is easily seen why, at certain periods when the conditions of the earth permitted, some species developed into monstrous and gigantic forms, which are no longer found. Lizards are still produced, and vary in form and size according to conditions; but we no longer find the gigantic saurians of the Jurassic Period.

VII

IS MAN THE SUMMIT OF EVOLUTION?

IT is a familiar criticism that there is nothing in the evolution theory to show that man is its ultimate product: he might be its latest, but not necessarily its last. If we assume that man has been developed from lowlier types by a certain process or by some unspecified cause, we may justly infer that the same agency can produce beings more highly evolved than man. And if we assume that the human intelligence has been evolved from very rudimentary beginnings, what limits can be set to the possibilities for the future? What sublime heights may not the human intellect attain? What marvelous powers may not some future being, evolved from ourselves, not be able to wield? If speculations of this kind should strike some minds as nonsense, and very capital nonsense, we decline to take the blame. We are merely trying to provide a logical sequence to the argument with which we are furnished; and if the whole existing animate creation has come forth from a jelly speck in a primeval sea, we see no particular reason why a great deal more should not come forth by the same method as the ages roll.

And it is indeed true that higher stages of evolution await the Spiritual Being who is now manifesting itself through the vehicle which we know as the ordinary man of today. To such higher stages we can only apply such names as Adepts, Masters of Wisdom, Initiates, Gods, Planetary Spirits; our language was not constructed with this in view, so the words may sound vague.

When we study our own consciousness, we realize that there is much more in us than has yet been unfolded; there is no reason for assigning limits to the possibilities of our attainment along these lines. As there comes to the very young child a moment when self-consciousness, the feeling of being a separate being, the power of contemplation of his own existence, dawns for the first time, so there may be in store for us another awakening to a still fuller self-realization. We shall then have passed the portals of initiation, and be no longer as other men. We shall have entered the 'Kingdom of Heaven.' Those forces in our own nature to which we are now subject will no longer have sway; and having thus become master in our own house, we shall become able to dispose of the forces of outside nature in a way in which the ordinary man of today cannot. We shall have what are called 'occult powers.' Here is one step in higher evolution. Our conscious perception will not be limited to the bounds set by the physical senses; our thoughts will not be centered on self, for the delusion of separateness will have been overcome. We may no longer need a physical body, but may use as our vehicle bodies of higher grades of matter.

But it is important to observe that this higher evolution is not confined to the future, except in the case of those beings who have not yet attained it. For the evolution of past cycles has already carried beings to these higher stages, and these may be called our elder brothers. Nor is it true that there has been a time when only lowly animals existed, followed by a time when higher animals appeared, and still later by man in his first appearance. There always have been all these grades, existing synchronously, each at its own particular stage of evolution. Such a statement may arouse questions as to whether there ever was a beginning or will ever be an end, and so forth; but such questions beset every inquiry, no matter what our theory may be, and should not be regarded as invalidating the position. Problems of infinity are beyond the scope of the intellect, at least in its present state, and it is not fair for a critic to oppose a theory on grounds of objection to which his own theory is at least equally liable.

VIII

ATAVISM

STUDENTS of heredity have observed the phenomenon known as atavism, which means the sudden reappearance in one generation of traits belonging to a remote generation and which have not shown themselves in the intermediate generations. Sometimes this is called reversion, and advocates of the evolutionary theories are fond of pointing to what they regard as traits of our savage ancestors or even of our arboreal ape ancestors, which crop out in civilized specimens of humanity. The facts are undeniable, but it does not follow that the explanation is right. Biology, with its materialistic interpretation, points to the existence, in the germinal cells, of elements which are passed on from generation to generation; and here we have at all events a physical interpretation of the phenomenon. But how much more significant does the matter become when viewed from the standpoint of Theosophy. That which is now man has existed in every lower form of organism, whether animal, vegetable, or what not; and consequently preserves rudiments of every one of those types. The mechanical explanation is ludicrously inadequate, for all this vast potentiality has to be loaded onto one microscopic physical speck. That speck is microscopic on the physical plane only; on the physical plane it is reduced to vanishing-point; but on other planes of matter, not less real because imperceptible to the physical senses, it is no microscopic speck. Let science explain on mechanical and physical principles how it is that memories of sixty years ago are still fresh and vivid in my mind as to be at times almost real.

It is evident that the physical mechanism does not suffice for an explanation; we must accept the idea that there are other grades of matter of finer structure than physical matter, and with properties unknown to physical science, which can serve as the storehouses for these latent impressions, and bring them forth into manifestation at particular times.

. . . man's *outward* shell passed through every vegetable and animal body before it assumed the human shape. — *The Secret Doctrine*, I, 282.

So atavism can be described as a form of memory; and somewhere in man's organism he carries all past experiences in the form of stored memory which under suitable conditions can be reproduced. Is it more wonderful than the fact that the voice of a speaker can be preserved on a disc or tape for an indefinite period, and be reproduced in exact detail for the benefit of auditors yet unborn?

What is known as 'recapitulation' means that the human foetus in the womb passes through a number of stages which more or less resemble the different types of animals; the evolutionists say that the foetus recapitulates the history of evolutionary stages preceding the human. There is such a recapitulation, but not in the sense which the evolutionists suppose. The developing human monad passes quickly through all the stages which that human monad has passed through in other cycles of evolution. For this monad, in far past ages, was accomplishing its evolution in the various kingdoms of nature, as plant and animal; and by a universal law it has to pass through these stages again from the beginning rapidly.

Every monad, whether in plant, animal, or even in the mineral atom, has originated in the human type and tends to revert to it.

. . . the human type is the repertory of all potential organic forms, and the central point from which these latter radiate. — *The Secret Doctrine*, II, 683

"*Every form on earth, and every speck (atom) in Space, strives in its efforts towards self-formation to follow the model placed for it in the* 'HEAVENLY MAN.' . . . *Its (the atom's) involution and evolution, its external and internal growth and development, have all one and the same object — man.*"—*Op. cit.*, I, 183

Everything that *is, was* and *will be*, eternally IS, even the countless forms, which are finite and perishable only in their objective, not in their *ideal* Form. They existed as Ideas, in the Eternity, and, when they pass away, will exist as reflections. Neither the form of man, nor that of any animal, plant or stone has ever been *created*, and it is only on this plane of ours that it commenced "becoming," *i. e.*, objectivising into its present materiality, or expanding *from within outwards,* from the most sublimated and supersensuous essence into its grossest appearance. Therefore *our* human forms have existed in the Eternity as astral or ethereal prototypes; according to which models, the Spiritual Beings (or Gods) whose duty it was to bring them into objective being and terrestrial Life, evolved the proto-plasmic forms of the future *Egos* from *their own essence.* After which, when this human *Upadhi,* or basic mold was ready, the natural terrestrial Forces began to work on those supersensuous molds *which contained, besides their own, the elements of all the past vegetable and future animal forms of this globe in them.*

— *Op. cit.,* I, 282

IX

INVOLUTION AND EVOLUTION

AS has been shown, evolution is neces-sarily a double process, for it means that a spirit or life-force is entering into something and causing that something to grow. The growing of the something is called evolution, and the passing of the spirit or life-force into it is called involution. The involution of spirit into matter causes the evolution of mater. The involution of mind into body causes the growth of body. The involution of life into an organism causes the evolution of the organism.

It will be observed that the word 'evolution' is unfortunately used in two different senses: (1) to denote the entire process; (2) to denote one phase of the process, involution being the other phase. As this ambiguous use of the word 'evolution' has became fixed, it is necessary to be on our guard against it.

It is evident that, if spirit involves into matter, so as to cause matter to evolve more and more, so that the matter expresses more and more of the qualities of the spirit, the process will eventually result in bringing things back to much the same state as they were in at first. Thus we can imagine steam being passed into water until at last all the water becomes steam. Thus the evolution is a continuous process, but cyclic, returning to a similar point. It is clear too that there must be a midway point, at which spirit and matter are equally balanced.

The process can thus be represented in the diagram of a circle, in which we consider the highest point as the beginning and the end. The lowest point, which is the midway point and is at the bottom, opposite to the beginning and end, represents a stage of evolution when the involution of spirit into matter has proceeded until the qualities of each are in equal proportions. In such a diagram the course of evolution is supposed to proceed down the left side and up the right side. The left side of the circle is known as the downward arc, the right side as the upward arc. During the progress of evolution along the downward arc, there is passage from spirituality to materiality, until the limit of materiality is reached at the lowest point; after which the ascending arc begins and there is progress from materiality towards spirituality. But it is to be noted that the whole process is a continual progress, and that the same power which causes spirit to descend into matter causes matter also to ascend into spirit; the one stage is a continuation of the other.

In the history of evolution it is taught that one great period of manifestation is called a

Manvantara, and that this is divided into seven Rounds, and each of these is subdivided into seven Root-Races. Our same diagram can be applied to the seven Rounds or to the seven Root-races. We are at present in the Fifth Root-Race of the Fourth Round. As 4 is the midway point of 7 stages, it is seen that we stand a little beyond the lowest point of materiality, and are on the ascending arc of evolution. We are aspiring away from materiality towards spirituality. While mankind was following the downward arc, in the earlier Root-Races, it was descending into matter; its path of self-realization lay in expressing itself more and more in matter. But our present path is different, as we have passed the midway point. So it is seen that what was right for humanity at one time may be wrong at another; if we were now to strive towards greater materiality, we should be turning backward against the course of evolution.

Thus far we have spoken of the involution of spirit into matter, and of the consequent evolution of matter into more spiritual forms. But this statement was only provisional, and was made for the sake of clarity. It needs modification; for it suggests that spirit and matter are two different and independent things, which is not the case. There is one universal Life, which manifests itself under the two aspects which we call spirit and matter, but these two aspects exist only by contrast with each other. A familiar illustration from physical science will make this point clear: suppose we were to compare the qualities of a liquid and a solid; we might call the liquid 'spirit,' and the solid 'matter'; but then, if we took a gas and a liquid, the gas would be spirit by contrast with the liquid, which would be matter. So what is spirit on one plane may be matter on the next higher plane; and spirit and matter, instead of being two distinct things are merely different grades of one thing. And so, in speaking of evolution, instead of saying that spirit descends into matter, it is more accurate to say that the one essence becomes gradually more material, and then again becomes more and more spiritual, until the cycle of evolution is accomplished.

X

CONCLUSION

THUS we have given some account of the leading features in our vast subject, and what we have tried to show is the laws that regulate change and growth throughout the universe, not merely the material universe, but also all those invisible realms that concern mind and spirit. Evolution is a conscious purposive process, and it is the work of living beings. The universe, in the last analysis, consists exclusively of living beings, and each and all of these are growing and evolving. Such a view necessarily makes the entire process exceedingly complex, and a complete understanding of it is not to be contemplated; but there is no limit to the advances which we can make in our knowledge of it by study and experience of life. The wise student will be willing to recognize the limitations of human faculty and the necessary degrees in its unfoldment; so that he will not suffer himself to be discouraged by impatience because he cannot grasp the whole subject at once.

APPENDIX
Note to page 32

Anatomical evidence of the primitiveness of the human stock, condensed from *Man in Evolution*, chapter viii, and largely taken from Dr. Wood-Jones, Professor of Anatomy in the University of London:

(1) The bones of the human skull articulate both at the base of the skull and on the sides of the brain-case in a manner characteristic of primitive mammalian animals; thus forming a marked contrast with the same articulations as found in the anthropoid apes and monkeys.

(2) The extreme primitive simplicity of the human nasal bones, in contrast with the case of the anthropoid and other simian stocks.

(3) In five respects in particular the skull is built on primitive mammalian lines, which have been departed from in some degree in all monkeys and apes: the back wall of the orbit, the metopic suture, the form of the jugal bone, the condition of the internal pterygoid plate, and the teeth.

(4) The human skeleton, especially in its variations, shows the same condition of primitive mammalian simplicity.

(5) As to the muscular system, man also retains many primitive features which have been lost in the rest of the Primates; among which are specially noted the pectoralis minor, whose attachment to the coracoid process is the original and primitive attachment, very

different from that of apes and monkeys, and still more so from that of many of the quadrupeds.

(6) The human tongue is primitive, and no ape or monkey has a tongue like the human.

(7) The vermiform appendix is strangely like that of some marsupials of Australia; it is very different in the apes and monkeys.

(8) The great arteries which arise from the arch of the aorta in man have the same number, are of the same kind, and are arranged in the same order as in the ornithorhynchus anatinus or duck-billed platypus of Australia. The apes and monkeys have not this arrangement.

(9) In man the premaxilla, the front part of the upper jawbone carrying the incisor teeth, does not exist as a separate element. But in apes, monkeys, and all other mammals, the premaxillary element is shown on the face by suture lines, outlining its junction with the maxillary bones.

Note to page 54
Quotations from Professor Bateson's address
at the Toronto meeting of the British Association, 1914.

"We have done with the notion that Darwin came latterly to favor, that large differences can arise from the accumulation of small differences. Such small differences are often mere ephemeral effects of conditions of life, and as such are not transmissible; but small differences, even when truly genetic, are factorial like the larger ones, and there is not the smallest reason for supposing that they are capable of summation."

"Examine any two thoroughly distinct species which meet each other in their distribution, as for instance Lychnis diurna and vespertina do. In areas of overlap are many intermediate forms. These used to be taken to be transitional steps, and the specific distinctness of

vespertina and diurna was on that account questioned.
Once it is known that these supposed intergrades are
merely mongrels between the two species, the transition
from one to the other is practically beyond our powers
of imagination to conceive."

"Knowledge of heredity has so reacted on our conception of variation that very competent men are
even denying that variation in the old sense is a genuine
occurance at all. Variation is postulated as the basis
of all evolutionary change. Do we then as a matter
of fact find in the world about us variations occurring
of such a kind as to warrant faith in a contemporary
progressive evolution? Till lately, most of us would
have said 'Yes' without misgiving."

"Distinct types once arisen, no doubt a profusion of
the forms called species have been derived from them
by simple crossing and subsequent recombination. New
species may now be in process of creation by this
means, but the limits of the process are obviously
narrow. On the other hand we see no changes in
progress around us in the contemporary world which
we can imagine likely to culminate in the evolution of
forms distinct in the larger sense. By intercrossing
dogs, jackals, and wolves new forms of these types can
be made, some of which may be species, but I see no
reason to think that from such material a fox could
be bred in indefinite time, or that dogs could be
bred from foxes."

"As we have got to recognise that there has been
an evolution, that somehow or other the forms of life
have arisen from fewer forms, we may as well see
whether we are limited to the old view that evolutionary progress is from the simplest to the complex, and
whether after all it is conceivable that the process
was the other way about."

For further information on this subject of Evolution consult:

THE ESOTERIC TRADITION — G. de Purucker, Vol I, pp. 305-339

THE MAHATMA LETTERS TO A. P. SINNETT (Consult Index)

MAN IN EVOLUTION — G. de Purucker

ARCHAIC HISTORY OF THE HUMAN RACE (Pamphlet compiled from *The Secret Doctrine* by G. van Pelt)

MANUALS IN THIS SERIES